Other Risks Include

Critical praise for Djelloul Marbrook's poetry

Far from Algiers (2008, Kent State University Press)

... as succinct as most stanzas by Dickinson... an unusually mature, confidently composed first poetry collection.
—Susanna Roxman, *Prairie Schooner* (author of *Crossing the North Sea*)

... brings together the energy of a young poet with the wisdom of long experience.
—Edward Hirsch, Guggenheim Foundation

... honors a lifetime of hidden achievement.
—Toi Derricotte, Stan and Tom Wick Poetry Prize judge, author of *Tender* and *The Undertaker's Daughter*

... wise and flinty poems outfox the Furies of exile, prejudice, and longing... a remarkable and distinctive debut.
—Cyrus Cassells, National Poetry Series winner

Brash Ice (2014, Leaky Boot Press, UK)

... a precision that occasionally recalls Yeats ...
—James Polk, *The Country and Abroad*

... aesthetically pleasing, thematically intriguing ...
—Michael Young, *The Poetry*

Brushstrokes and glances (2010, Deerbrook Editions)

Whether it is commentary on state power, corporate greed, or the intensely personal death of a loved one, Djelloul Marbrook is clear-sighted, eloquent, and precise. As the title of the collection suggests, he uses the lightest touch, a collection of fragments, brushstrokes and glances, to fashion poems that resonate with truth and honesty.
—Phil Constable, *New York Journal of Books*

... looks at art the way a drinker drinks—deeply, passionately, and desperately, as if his life depended on it ... makes you want to run out to your favorite museum and look again, as you have never looked before, until the lights go out.
—Barbara Louise Ungar, author of
Thrift; *Charlotte Bronte, You Ruined My Life*; *The Origin of the Milky Way*

... one of those colossal poets able to bridge worlds—poetry and art, heart and mind—with rare wit, grace, and sincerity; a soft-spoken artist with the courage to face the "fatal beckoning" of his muse ... crisp intellect, seamlessly interwoven with loss and longing. ... poetry at its best: at once both gritty and refined, private and political, tender and tough as iron ... well worth reading.
—Michael Meyerhofer, author of
What to do if you're buried alive, *Damnatio Memoriae*, *Blue Collar Eulogies*

...delicately wrought... highly recommended reading...because, ultimately, this witness so clearly loves his subject.
—Eileen Tabios, Editor, *Galatea Resurrects*

Riding Thermals to Winter Grounds (2017, Leaky Boot)

... some very powerful lines, such as: "And then, near the end of my life, I become the man I wanted to be without the fuss and bother of giving a damn."
—Sidney Grayling, Editor, Onager Editions

Shadow of the Heron (2016, Coda Crab Books)

A 21st-century Blake—reconciling innocence and experience—Marbrook urges the contemporary reader to retreat to the quiet of unknowing, to live "in dusks of mirrors," where our truest selves can find their reflections.
—Dean Kostos, Benjamin Saltman Award for *This Is Not a Skyscraper*

༄

Critical praise for Djelloul Marbrook's fiction

Artemisia's Wolf (title story, *A Warding Circle*, 2017, Leaky Boot)

... Djelloul Marbrook's impressive novella ... successfully blends humor and satire (and perhaps even a touch of magic realism) into its short length ... an engrossing story, but what might strike the reader most throughout the book is its infusion of breathtaking poetry ... a stunning rebuke to notoriously misogynist subcultures like the New York art scene, showing us just how hard it is for a young woman to be judged on her creative talent alone.
—Tommy Zurhellen, *Hudson River Valley Review*

Saraceno

Djelloul Marbrook writes dialogue that not only entertains with an intoxicating clickety-clack, but also packs a truth about low-life mob culture "The Sopranos" only hints at. You can practically smell the anisette and filling-station coffee.—
Dan Baum, author of *Gun Guys* (2013), *Nine Lives: Mystery, Magic, Death and Life in New Orleans* (2009), and others

...a good ear for crackling dialogue ... I love Marbrook's crude, raw music of the streets. The notes are authentic and on target ...

—Sam Coale, *The Providence* (RI) *Journal*

... an entirely new variety of gangster tale ... a Mafia story sculpted with the most refined of sensibilities from the clay of high art and philosophy ... the kind of writer I take real pleasure in discovering ... a mature artist whose rich body of work is finally coming to light.

—Brent Robison, editor, *Prima Materia*

Alice Miller's Room (title story, *Making Room,* 2017, Leaky Boot)

Marbrook lets his powerful imagination run wild, leading the fiction into unexpected corners where weird performers hold court and produce endings that both astonish and are frequently magical.

—James Polk, contributing editor, *Art/World*

This enchanting novella is a delicately wrought homage to Jung's famous principle of meaningful coincidence...

—*Breakfast All Day,* UK

... the story draws us into that mysterious and terrifying realm where the heart will have its say and all who enter leave transformed...

—Dr. Patricia L. Divine, Head Start program national award winner

Mean Bastards Making Nice (2014, Leaky Boot)

I love it. I admire it. It is you at your best.

—Novelist Gail Godwin on "The Pain of Wearing Our Faces"

Guest Boy (2018, Leaky Boot)

... it is in books like this that I seek answers and guidance as I travel my own path to enlightenment and contentment. This book opened a struggle in me...

—Isla McKetta, editor, *A Geography of Reading*

Other Risks Include

poems by
Djelloul Marbrook

LEAKY BOOT PRESS

Other Risks Include
by Djelloul Marbrook

Acknowledgments

"Earth's disease" was published by *Le Zaparogue* in 2014.

"Some Cordoba in my mind" was published in late 2017 by *Indifaring Muse*, a publication of Vishwabharati Research Center in India.

First published in 2018 by
Leaky Boot Press
http://www.leakyboot.com

Copyright © 2018 Djelloul Marbrook
All rights reserved

No part of this book may be reproduced or transmitted in any form or by any means, electronic, mechanical, photocopying, recording, or otherwise, without prior written permission of the author.

ISBN: 978-1-909849-23-5

In rare cases death may not occur for some months.

*For my aunt, Dorothy Rice,
and my grandmother, Hilda Waterman Rice.
They saved me.*

Contents

Proem

As if my species   17

Other risks include

Except as a protocol   21
Earth's disease   22
The most dangerous day   23
The edgeless puzzle   24
Incredible aperture   25
A reading   26
I may need a thimble   27
Forty times that of wolves   29
Presence   30
Can't remember the sonofabitch   31
Clear cache escape program help   32
Violet light under chanterelle   33
Do-re-mi   34
All there would be   35

The burned-out engine

The burned-out engine of something divine   39
Thirteen naked lines   40
I throw my soul down the stairs   41
I have a raven's sense of being watched   42
Scutch and chisel   43
Avoidance   44
Some Cordoba in my mind   45

Rip Van Winkle Bridge	46
Enter the eye in cold blood	47
Bowling heads	48
No walking back the story	49
We too have died	50
Entrails of our glitterings	51
What's left	52
Equations	53

Dumbstruck

I take wing dumbstruck	57
The last time I saw Lois	59
Squall	60
Dead	61
Difference	62
Unless it tells me	63
Confederate	64
Cicada din	65
Breakup of the Soviet Union	66

All is a shard

Shards	69
Plot	70
Paradise	71
Watching crows	72
The low growl of my stare	73
Rather than my mother's breathing	74
Nine hundred feet a second	75

Rather than be artists

Rather than be artists	79
Love poem	80
Do we forgive?	81
Viaticum	82
Tomorrow I'm going on a tear	83
This kiln of recollection	85
Al Niffari	86

Tarn	87
Time to make up stories	88
I saw Ilium	89
The happy inheritor	90
Gronk	91
Tumbling churches	93
I don't know, I sense	94
Withstood	95

Proem

As if my species

Other risks include
encountering me one summer day
wearing the suit I was buried in
possible tremors
which may become permanent
if you insist on prizing cracks
and death may result
from swiveling your head too fast
to see me studying you
as if my species
needed the intelligence
call your doctor immediately
if the feeling persists
I'm living in your attic
and you were born
under a mushroom
picketed by hellebore in the rain
and when you're done with me
or I'm done with you
and the rite of spring
has insured another solstice
may we
not heed the warning signs
or do anything about
this dread disease
for which we spend our lives
inventing names.

Other risks include

Except as a protocol

No television here, we're dying.
Wave off the nurse and the priest,
it all comes down to the ICU,
all that seemed too much to bear,
all that seemed too much to bare,
becomes so little now
as to be an annoyance,
and there isn't even time
to imagine life annoying
all those anonymous whoms.
Which of us gives a whom
and can we really survive
the loss of this memory palace?
I say we only think we can
but none of us leaves this room
alive in any sense of the word
except as a protocol.

Earth's disease

I am a cathode ray tube,
a particle accelerator;
look at me, I change you.
Nothing drains me more
than what I long to happen.

These things you want to happen,
help earth shake off
the toxins of your desire,
take their names from them,
their anchor rodes—cut them.

This is all death is, not
to be foolish anymore,
not to cling to notions
that are more heartless than
the enemies you loved.

We are the earth's disease;
its triumph is to live with us.
All a little pity would be
is to want less and take
more responsibility.

The most dangerous day

The day you're born is the day you're most likely
to be murdered.
Some sense of that must linger, some sense
that all is not luck,
some sense trust is both risk and fakery,
and far from danger past
the first day is a foreboding that might survive the last day,
foreboding that the world exists in the peripheral glance
and everything we grasp is illusion and fairy tale.

Call it chagrin to celebrate that first day
and the insult of a name,
chagrin to wear in secret places,
to show like a bared tooth,
an untoward smile. We know we did not survive
and are golems
in search of the living, and if we find them
what are we to do
or say? Make art, tear down civilizations,
join cabals and sing.
Or is it possible to enter and inhabit
that peripheral glance?

The edgeless puzzle

As for the edgeless puzzle,
since that most dangerous day
working from the center out,
I found no further ends,
damned good science since
the universe expands.
They handed it to me
in a measles-darkened room,
pieces missing, others crazed,
and I pretended it was okay
so not to offend do-gooders,
if that's how it was going to be.
Here was my little subversion,
I wasn't going to freeze-frame
Peter Rabbit for the McGregors
in the asylum, not me.
That was my racer's edge,
working on the razor,
splitting the difference
with an indifferent world.

Incredible aperture

I'm not on a deadline, I'm on beloved time,
sickness of health, surfeit of wealth,
time of no telling, incredible aperture.

No counting on anything but love & ignorance,
which is a pinhole of hope, a reason to wake up
and watch the next damned thing tumble
from the second hand of the clock of conceit.

What did I understand not subject to belief? I understood
that when I thought someone owed me the truth
I was shut off from it. I understood
truth was in the pupil of my eye and that light
must be let in, and all that I ever did on time
is nothing compared to there always being time
to let celestial berserkers in.

We could not rape or murder each other
but for the tyranny of time,
so when I took off my wristwatch,
my name bracelet and ring, I began the larger project
of rubbing off my name from possession, the larger project
of being possessed by namelessness.

A reading

> Bless what does not come off,
> a doorknob, a heart attack,
> a reward . . .

Your fly is open
& you remind the girl in the front row
of someone she wants dead

> . . . a burglary of hearts,
> a raid on the premises
> on which we live.

The man in the third row
sees you brushing death aside;
he's ill of wishing you ill.

> Oh yes, like my mother.
> Bless what does not come off,
> even a mother's love.

I may need a thimble

I want to push a needle through a rolled-up rubber band,
 that's a stripped-down version of my ambition,
  something an old man can accomplish
   if nothing to brag about on Facebook.

I notice your speech is slurred;
are you on something?

 Onto something and the slur as you call it
  is the musical intuition of melancholy.

Whatever that means.

 Precisely.

 I may need a thimble as I did long ago
when I sewed polar bear skins with a three-sided needle.
 Leopard skins are softer, sheep very soft,
but polar bear skins brought out the Frankenstein in me,
 imbued me with a towering ambition
  to put matters together again
   as if life were taxidermy
 and I slept among the glistening beasts.

Mothballs were your coughdrops,
benzine your hair tonic
and nothing escaped your glass eyes
especially what you pretended not to see

                    but now I see all that matters
              is a sculpture no one will let be....

a defiance as relevant as you want it to be.

                                I haven't decided.

Do we really know the point at which we die?
Would a living man aspire to needle a rubber band?

Forty times that of wolves

I couldn't be distracted from the cracks
by the way they rode the platelets around
flying gonfalons and firing cannons,
their rhetoric worse than war, triumphalism
metastasizing until they were dying of it,

and they noticed that even in the crib
my gaze fixed on the blackness between
their continents of hubris, noticed and abhorred
this inhuman child, this dropping
of a passing daemon, this leaving

who sat too still and saw too much,
this summoner of wraiths, this bomber
of theaters whose olfactory sense
was forty times that of wolves,
whose eyes frisked their most impregnable parts.

I couldn't be distracted from the cracks
from which the next galaxy would expand,
the one to which some of us are born in touch
reeking of it as if by some wrong turn
we happened here while playing with our friends.

Presence

They took out my heart and put it in my hand.
But how will I live? You never needed it, they said,
but now romantics will try to inhabit you,
creatures with no respect for facts.
How will I live without a pulse? You will
live as well as you have without facts,
better even, because you won't be deafened
by your desires, and for the first time
you will hear others and you will recognize
that elusive presence you have been yammering about.

Can't remember the sonofabitch

dropped clear out of my mind
heard it clatter down the well
who was what he said & how
could I forget considering
I remember migratory patterns
& mutterings of millions of bad ideas

sailing mud puddles in Mexico
I'll haul him up from the well
cut out his heart on a pyramid
and send it to his wife if
I can remember her name
& if not, eat it with shallots & parsley

that's the trouble with
fading in & out of lives as if
they were consciousness
and what's not is rest
or something like a prayer
in the lost gardens of Az Zahra

don't ever say let it never be said
because it's going to be said
by poets, murderous priests
& other gargoyles from whose minds
we plummet & live lives listening
to the cries and echoes of our fall

Clear cache escape program help

I knew a man who died crying for help
help I always knew was a slight alteration
in a glow of a facet of the amplitudhedron
so I waited patiently in the driveway
for the family that had business elsewhere
and I wondered if that shining place
required a disguise and could I acquire
such a disguise and what would I be hiding
and one day I realized it was my deadly clarity
and I didn't want to give it up which meant
the sort of life I've lived in the driveway

Violet light under chanterelle

All that I missed is echinacea,
medicinal, not to be confused
with where my life was heading
and above all not to be regretted
because its shimmering arrests
the signaling of disappointment,
and that enables me to progress
to violet light under mushrooms,
songs of chanterelle and secrets
I have already taken with me,
and now I'm looking down at me,
mopping up, lifting a glass to things
I did well in spite of expectations
sewn over me like a shroud.

Goodbye, dear friend, and thank you
for preferring shimmering to them.

Do-re-mi

Don't tell me some vital part
like air conditioning or the brain
is going to break down in the middle
of an orgy of recognition
of a self taking shape & all
the work we've done will spoil
waiting for repairs don't tell me
I'm going to spin against a wall
of ordinariness just when
the sublime is tickling my nose
& I'm about to sneeze a storm
to swamp the fleet of circumstance
& establish me as a demigod
of do-re-mi & silliness
under minarets of gibberish
don't tell me I've been a blind mullah
all along & must retire
to a fungal cave in oolalong
fumbling my beads
& preparing for the Mahdi
or even becoming him
in some final irony

All there would be

She is beautiful in a perilous way
as if not meant to enjoy herself
but to trip the wires to which we're rigged

I first encountered her in a maze—
we sipped air tea in tin cups
and understood this is all there would be,

the rest would be the getting home
filled with the debris we threw before us
and bombs we couldn't resist setting off

The burned-out engine

The burned-out engine of something divine

No security checks are required

The trams run on time
over the nine circles of hell

The tyranny of morality
should have made an exception of lust
to celebrate nothing but now
to spit in the politician's face
to shit on the altar of doctrine

Nothing is immortal but this
outcome of all equations
that finally we have the decency to observe
and observing
this grasp of a door handle
this exchange of glances
this gasp
we come to understand
how many times we have lived

Thirteen naked lines

for Susan Aberth

Can't sing for long can't stay for long
but in the glade of interlocking circles
from behind an ash I've watched the sacred rites
of our companions and know how much depends
on the tolerance of fools
This is the land of partial eclipse
where stranger than syzygy events
spin out from under our feet and words
refuse to be broken on the wheel and sold
and no one who has stood in sol niger light
will ever be drawn to the scent
of a human again
Can't sing for long or stay forlorn

I throw my soul down the stairs

disguised as a blue shirt, a wall
opens for it, I exult, heedless
of what happens next. This is the way
I want to live the rest of it even if
it's only a moment long. How long
is a moment, how long does it take
for me to care? Goodbye shirt,
goodbye soul, goodbye color blue,
I'm standing at the head of the stairs
waiting for the apocalypse,
and as usual I'm not bored.

I have a raven's sense of being watched

I fly off over the heaths of my brain
studying the shadows of my thoughts
pleased not to be an exhibitionist
and yet annoyed because I was doing something
which now I forget
that ought not to have been disturbed
by someone's molesting look

I fly straight at him or her I don't know which
and rather than sounding like a human scream
I shit like a human bomber in my contempt
at having been felt up
by such an idle curiosity

Scutch and chisel

Scutch chisel rasp and riffle I carve faces
for invisible companions to enthuse
and of their fallen features make
architects of graphene cities
floating on titanic water lilies
worshipping the sun
as if it were a navel or a pore
of Artemis too vast to see
carve faces with so sharp a glance
their excesses fall to talc leaving
intent so naked it would shame
all but a child wise enough to know
he is too subversive to be allowed
to grow up

Avoidance

He didn't want to dive into poison ivy
so he let the hunter shoot him

That's my academic history
the whole of what I know about avoidance
and I would have bled out
were it not for a certain stillness in me
that knew better than
to what?

Tell me, tell me before I get up to go

Some Cordoba in my mind

I've attended this university for eighty years
and leave without that degree
of savvy necessary to survive such a savage place
I enfold my books in a baseball jacket
and leave them on a bench
in front of the library
in hope of finding the subway
remembering my name
and where I live which seems so distant
I'd need another eighty years to get there
I've always gone by subway
subvert subject subsume way
to some Cordoba in my mind
where I'll rest to be prepared
better than I was for this

Rip Van Winkle Bridge

What is there better than this
walking across the Rip Van Winkle Bridge?

What survives this cold
this red-scarved day?

Fame? Glory?
Love of morality's tyranny?
Some slippery-footed hope
some fulfillment somewhere I forget?

I had ideas once of better things.

I'm glad they've blown away
and that I am the bridge
for the child lost to his mother,
from one dream to another.

Enter the eye in cold blood

wear blaze orange look-at-me all to hell
I look only until my pupils narrow and then
take stock of the all too much I have let in
I am my well-governed aperture kindly
only to what eludes and does not allude
to this and that showy things & godlings
enter the eye in cold blood and must be warmed
by our affections a precarious fate
I would not wish on those whom I have loved

Bowling heads

In an eight-carat orgy of light
I bowl the heads I've worn
at creatures memories become
desperately glad to see them
clearer than when I was drunk on them
they splatter electric trees
in neon fury at being known
and said and done beyond repair
I was their foreigner now they're mine
and we have less to say
than that dishonesty then
more than golems ask to go away

No walking back the story

No way back
from the creatures we encounter
from their black holes
and implosions within ourselves
no way back but the lie
that we did not see
and were not there
no back there
no walking back the story
until it is untold
in the utter chaos
of the pupil fully dilated
and the moment backlit
by the world's burning ruins

We too have died

We don't know which ones are dead
we can't tell by their light
but the distance it travels
lightens our bones
and we take heart
in their similarity to us
because we too have died and live on
sending our messages
across the darkness
to the semblances
in which we now live

Entrails of our glitterings

The grandest erections are infested by rats
our stories their facades and skyscrapers
plague-bearers scuttling hole to hole
in the entrails of our glitterings
& we are what we choose not to see
more than what we do
& so much more than what we own
because possession goes to ruin
in the corner of the eye
& and that is why few of us are gainly
& most of us catch our feet
on doorsills of the brightest day
& hear rats scuttering behind us
see snake tails vanishing
in the stone fences up ahead

What's left

Scrub out the sheen of getting along—
anger, beguiling and true,
runs a finger across your palm
and says let's get out of here,
let's go somewhere quiet
to flirt with calamity, or
if we turn each other on
we might pursue honesty
to its most dangerous possibility
undo our parents' expectations
and our own, and unmask
our most successful faces.

Then in our deadly nakedness
we might inventory what's left.

Equations

I don't now what to do about this
tsunami of recognitions but swim
through debris with snakes
& then recede to that horizon
where it's possible to sleep
& not be jammed up by wherewithals
ampersands & asterisks not
be hampered by the querulousness of things
I don't know what to do about this
& that is closer than I've ever come
to becoming one of the great equations

Dumbstruck

I take wing dumbstruck

A white egret stands in the negative
inviting me to occupy her soul

she can't move for fear
it would profane with color
all that is to be undone

If I would be staying longer
I'd build a gazebo over there
and put a rowboat in the pond

shadows darken the mountain

I'm in a hurry to become
a bench in Central Park
a high note of someone's song
a particle of your carbon self
a speck in Antares' eye
a canticle of hard dismay
a killing frost

seemed like forever
and now it's here
something that once seemed so remote
comes a hundred lives at once
to make a positive

my complaints are dandelions
pick them make wine

I will not be a figure eight
lying on its side
in the grasp of a great Norway

lights prick the shadow
on the mountainside

I stand in my proper estate
and take wing dumbstruck

The last time I saw Lois

she was staring into the abyss
I was superfluous & saw
her as the faery light of dreams
I wanted her
to tell me how to want
not to go away
where all I wanted went
a privacy
where impostors like me
were forbidden

The last time I saw Lois
I became a hair
in the sights of irrelevance

Life is goodbye
& muted utterance
after being dumbstruck

Squall

My rib has popped a cleat
from this floating dock of a body
to follow Monarchs and hummingbirds
to Mexico, to the pyramids of Yucatan,
and I am bleeding internally
the blood that drowns my memories.
My seacock opens to the possibilities
of the amniotic sea. I am scuttled
in plain view of foundering angels.

Dead

They're not sentimental about us,
being dead not only to us
but to our beliefs. My mother told me so
when I put a white rose on her stone.

They see how we lose our shoes
in a muck of fears and walk on
over broken dogma bleeding.
They taste our bloody tracks,

lick the stones of our grief
and don't care how we dishonor
or honor them too much.
We fail to bemuse them.

Difference

the difference between looking in and looking out
is being someone's child and no one's child

between attracting hummingbirds
and ill-makers on the wind

I move in the difference
hoping death is an adoption
of a mistaken child

Unless it tells me

You who know where to put things,
I might be one of those things, so
how should I trust you? I might
even be your repository. How
do you know we're not laughing at you
for thinking our names contain us
or anything is contained?

I don't know where anything belongs
and I believe it unlawful to insist,
not by the opinions of lawyers
or the conventions of nations,
but by instincts known to astronomers.
I don't know where anything belongs.
Orderliness is a flawed equation.

Confederate

My particles tried this and that
in their frenzy to belong,
then one day they thought any shape
better suited their dignity,
and that can hardly be good
for the decisions I make.
I don't know what they're going to say
or do or faintly resemble
but it can't be half as bad as worrying.
My particles tried this and that
before I signed the articles
of confederation, and now
it hardly matters what takes shape
since each of them reserves
the right to secede
from the contraption of the whole,
and me, I reserve the right to recede
from the political mess
my great desire to belong
made of youthful prospects.

Cicada din

Straggly, hungering for the sun,
our heads weigh us down,
to shroud the cicadas.
We are trampled for our quest,
made to think we overstepped,
but in the cicada din we hear
drums summoning us
to reach out again
to what we were convinced
we didn't see, to embrace
the dangers of second sight.

Breakup of the Soviet Union

My body soviet breaks up
in no telling how many parts,
its song-dependent economy
debates the nature of silence.
I wake up talking gibberish,
my mother tongue forgotten.
I fall off ladders cursing gravity.
My one remaining allegiance
disappears. I forget my name.

All is a shard

Shards

All is a shard of something else,
hope gone bleak, ecstasy,
a glance, a gasp, a scent, a glimpse
under a leaf, rust that was
bright. Nothing that we see
is just the name we gave it.
Going downtown is a great sea voyage,
a lilting step, a flight, arms
outspread in consecration.
We don't know where we are,
we're only where we say we are,
and in every shadow, behind
every plank and tree a tragedy
and a triumph unfold equally.

Plot

Dreams disorder our genes,
no one is as the night before

Every untoward & rogue glance
is the plot that enraptures us

What are we to do about this crime
we have witnessed in each other

now that we know we cannot know
who we are or what we've done

by consenting to be human
in spite of forensic evidence

there were other beasts to be
in places better than this galaxy?

Paradise

He wanted to photograph his clasped hands
looking down on them like a raven
but he needed them to do it

This conundrum could drive me mad
he said with such delight he knew
he had already been driven there

there where such things matter
the laws of physics could be remade
and nothing that we need be denied us

where the artist enters the painting
and sends a doppelganger home
to pay the rent and face the music

Watching crows

Hard to wash off the soil of disdain,
petty meanness and spite;
they do metastasize,
and yet we are somewhat immune
if only we can love to see the hurt
before it makes a nest of us.
And how would we do that?
I think by watching crows
drawn to whatever grows.

The low growl of my stare

sends back the man of parts
to confer with Dr. Frankenstein
about proprieties. I sniff
ten thousand odors, his
fills me with the sorrow
of finding oneself here again.
To have manufactured him
in Onan not by coitus
but sheer will of one, was it
more evil than having sex
to make another one
of a kind that rapes and murders?
I know this monster better
than I ever knew my friends,
he might as well be me
for all I've ever been human.

Rather than my mother's breathing

in a hospital of their kind
I heard how many years I would live
as a murmuration in forsythia
& a line of Arabic in the sky:
tomorrow there are none,
but I don't squander me in sleep
because dreams are alternatives—
didn't I get here by waking up too soon?

Nine hundred feet a second

what's a hollow point compared
to piloted drones of the mind,
compulsions to derail
& decouple, chemical spills,
calamities within that wait
to put on the skits we call
reality because we're afraid
that in ourselves we'll find
cures which for there's no disease,
dimensions in cracks of walls,
astronomies beyond dogma & religion.

Nine hundred feet a second,
bullets are the least of what's coming at us;
starlight, malevolence & desires
pin us like butterflies,
but no lepidopterist can count
on our being there in the morning
because we're stranger than graphene,
as volatile as love but not
predictable. We're too strange
to inhabit our skin and won't
look like this for long, as wild turkeys
no longer look like dinosaurs.

Rather than be artists

Rather than be artists

What if it were up to us to color things,
to stretch canvas, apply tempera,
what if it were up to us to arrange the forms,
to arrest expressions? It is up to us,
but we prefer to be buyers, patrons
of someone else's pain. What if white balance
abandoned us to our devices and panic
usurped the job of black? Where
would we stand in regard to this?
Are we the painting or the painter
or raw material waiting
for decisions we die to make?
More is up to us than we are up to.
Dolphins and roaches will outlive us
because we wrap each moment in dogma
to suffocate it rather than be artists.

Love poem

white cells rush to my face
in abhorrence of you

my hard disk sputters
and chucks your words into the gutter

my body gutters at the thought
of your touch

I like ecstatic mouths
incapable of smirk
and should have told you that
instead of encouraging you to think
I am your patriot

but I was young and needy
for everything but moment
and now I'm old and know
that is all there is

Do we forgive?

Who forgives us
for noticing
they have no soul?
They use no scalpels
the true surgeons
cut with a look
a word. Our scars
mean to disabuse
cold surgeons
of our resentments
but we remember
what they took
to pay their bills.
They sell our parts
to buy respite.
Do we forgive
ourselves for noticing?

Viaticum

Two smirky excommunicators up your holy arse,
five buggerers to wholly see your canon,
as many lice as your confession will hold,
twelve red caps to process your bullshit home,
and all the liturgy notwithstanding,
the smoke, Nosferatus at the altar and child abuse,
the ecstasy, magnificence and glory,
all will be transfigured by the itch
for oneness that eludes everyone but heretics.
Their heresies, no matter what their naked warts,
will prevail for their sheer anathema
and every kind of perversion signal
the selection of another menace to society.
Two nuns will open up a little auto-da-fé
on the rue Viaticum to serve the hackers
who rattle the model that failed to consider time.

Tomorrow I'm going on a tear

I may spell it differently
by the time I'm done.
It will be like the church's silence
about the Sermon on the Mount.
It will be a shaken vial,
my forefinger stopping it
as long as it takes to spell *when*
and then I will happen
against the odds of being born,
happen like red skies at morning,
not as forecast, aberrant
and above all needing—
above it, I say, my shield banging
on the gunwale as I approach
another damned smugness
passing for a monastery.
Never mind about the nuns
and the chalices, I'm after
the moment when there's a tear
in the blue veil of illusion,
nothing I can stuff in a great hall
or drown in a grinning goblet
or braid in a maiden's hair,
but another way to spell and be spelled
by a tear I'm going on to shed.

Then I'll part the styrofoam
on the black sea of memory
to point the longboat home
crackling and alight with glee.

This kiln of recollection

Legacy is what doesn't clean up.
When I go back into the house
it doesn't matter which house
I know I will be interrupted
tearing ampersands of myself
down in closets stinking
of instances I failed to meet,
interrupted by devils whose injured tails
rebuke my club-footedness.
Please excuse my ghostliness;
I'm trying to carry it all away
but specific rooms crawling
with their conflated moments
hide behind my new illusions.
To find my way out I tie
a rope of poems around me
like a high priest entering
the holy of holies which turns out to be
this kiln of recollection.
There is hardly enough of me
left to burn, enough perhaps
to inspire a firefly.

Al Niffari

Mercury is stuck in somebody's hut
and I'm seriously retrograde,
pregnant with a yen
that feels like someone's disease,
incurably irrelevant
to what's happening here,
pharmaceutically indifferent
to the spelling of now,
mathematically insane,
yet somehow determined to deliver
a stone not yet in my possession
to the dock of my regression
on the Sea of Honoria
in the coming age of calm.

Tarn

And then nothing ever happened
or, being nothing, could have been,
but as I waited for it to happen
I found peace in becoming part of it,
becoming it as it was becoming to me,
and all my restlessness stood
in front of me as someone else's stress,
someone uprising from the bottom
of a glacial tarn, not exactly a former self
but a person no one wanted me to be,
a drowned person consenting to be me.
Not exactly did I weight him down
and row away, not exactly was I myself,
and now I celebrate this inexactly because
it is the trysting glade of ghosts.

Time to make up stories

We think the pupa in the pupil
is the last face seen on earth,
but it's our companion's face
releasing us from our promise
to endure so that after this
nothing is under oath and may
happen to us indecently
in a heaven worth imagining.

The eye is fog at birth
to give our new custodians
time to make up stories
about the doll in the sphere
to brace themselves against the horror
of the irresistible glance into the abyss.

The pupa reminds us earth is a speck
in a firmament so vast
we would rather be dolls
than the shape-shifters we are.

Companions curl around us
inhabiting this, that and who,
training us to disappear
and we know our desire to be seen
is the measure of our fear.

I saw Ilium

The trees
I climbed to see
Babylon
and Woodstock
are gone
to make a table
and keep
someone warm.

Who
survives
such calamities?

I saw Ilium
and never wanted
to come ashore
to life
and death
and literature.

The happy inheritor

I would like to look at trees
and know what they're talking about
I would like to ply the civilizations in a stone
I would like to be on good terms with the ocean's secrets
I would like to die in good odor with snipers
who had me in their crosshairs but relented
and leave as the happy inheritor
of at least a few of the other lives I've lived

Gronk

Anxious to hear me?
I think some dogs were
but nothing warmed me
from the dread
on people's faces.

Sitting on a dolphin
I emit a gronk
when I would have sung
with bellbuoys
if wraiths would hear me.

I'm tired of my head
damming up the witness
of my eyes. My feet are numb
from waiting for directions
that never come.

Finding a doorknob in the dark
is something to celebrate;
if it comes off in your hand
pity the door for its hole,
let the mad light in.

If I had better advice
I'd be tried for treason;
as it is, I'm serving time
in the salvage of words,
feeling up their parts.

Dorian Gray is about a cardinal sin:
holding one's share in the maelstrom
of ideas, an act of supreme distrust,
something like religion, dark,
song splattered on a wall.

Tumbling churches

A confession not made is dew
in the pubic sky and scent
of wisdom retained

lightning bugs wink
at the sleepless and unbeguiled
and their thunderous beds tumble churches

I don't know, I sense

I'm not tall enough,
my mouth's not big enough
to live. The alternative
is always what I choose
and it's not, no, it's not
what you think it is.
It's life somewhere else
where these issues don't arise
because delight, delight
is the only enterprise.

Withstood

I am
that I am
withstood
in spite of myself
a poem
burning on a palette
in the gale
of reluctant miracle
a message
a witness
that pebbles
& scuttling leaves
are not incidental
I am
that I am in behalf
of them
that in stars' cosmic latté
nothing is a lie
nothing a dream

www.ingramcontent.com/pod-product-compliance
Lightning Source LLC
LaVergne TN
LVHW041548070426
835507LV00011B/988